MW01194911

AN INSTRUCTIONAL MANUAL
FOR ENTREPENEURS
AND HOBBYISTS

THIS MANUAL WILL HELP YOU SEE

AND UNDERSTAND HYDROPONICS

IN A NEW LIGHT.

"Planting a seed and growing it to maturity is one of the most satisfying things a man can do for his soul."

- Author Unknown

THE SECRET OF

NON-CIRCULATING

HYDROPONICS

AN INSTRUCTIONAL

MANUAL FOR

ENTREPENEURS & HOBBYISTS

TERRY MOORE CADLE

The Secret of

Non-Circulating Hydroponics

This book may not be reproduced in whole or in part by any means, without permission.
For information address:
information@hydro-grow.net; Specimen Plants LLC;

FORWARD

It was on the Big Island of Hawaii that I first learned about the idea of non-circulating hydroponics. I attended a semester series of classes in 1994, at the University of Hawaii , Hilo, taught by Dr. Bernard Kratky, which included visiting various nurseries on the Big Island who were growing in hydroponics. The commercial flower growers were always researching updated methods and trying alternative crop solutions to combat the ever increasing blights and fungus they were subject to, which required more alternative methods. Having spent over ten years in the nursery business on the Big Island, growing was something I did well and wanted to continue to do even though I was moving back to Florida. I was ready for something new. This opportunity began a succession of trials and successes that led to the commercial enterprise featured in this book. This method was so inexpensive, yet was effective and successful on a large scale. This system was originally developed for areas of islands and locations where electric costs were high and water in short supply. It will be increasingly more valuable as these costs continue to rise for everyone.

Florida was a great place to set up the nursery, however getting through each summer was always inventive. We devised methods of cooling the greenhouses and imported beneficials to help with some of the pests. It's great to see hydroponics growing into the bigger industry it is today. I see other non-circulating methods being used which also seem to be as effective. Compared to the costs of installing lines and pumps, growers need to consider these methods, which are a fraction of the costs of circulating hydroponics and equally as successful.

Bill Cadle

Bill's Lettuce
Vero Beach, FL

TABLE OF CONTENTS

Many thanks to Dr. Bernard Kratky, without whom this growing enterprise and teaching manual would not have been possible.

THE SECRET OF NON-CIRCULATING HYDROPONICS

An easy to follow guide

to alternative hydroponics.

INTRODUCTION

Welcome to the wonderful world of non-circulating hydroponics. This manual will provide you with the necessary information to help you design, build and implement an incredibly low-cost, low-maintenance hydroponic system. The simplicity of this hydroponics method has been largely overlooked by mainstream hydroponics. Without expensive pumps and accessories, it's easy to see why. As progressive growers become aware of this effective, cost reducing method, mainstream hydroponics and agriculturalists in general will accept its validity and welcome its viability. More importantly, average house-holders, living in small spaces, will begin to utilize this technique, providing fresh, unadulterated produce for their own families and friends and additional income for themselves. The incredible diversity this system affords will complement any lifestyle. Upon completion of this manual, you will have all the information necessary to successfully build and implement your own hydroponic growing system. Enjoy your gardening and this introduction to non-circulating hydroponics. Following these simple instructions you will begin a growing adventure that could change your life.

A STORY OF HYDROPONICS

Hydroponics date back as long ago as 580BC. In the dry arid plains of southeastern Iraq, King Nebuchadnezzar II designed one of the Seven Wonders of the World, the Hanging Drip Gardens of Babylon. These magnificently constructed series of terraces were approximately one hundred feet across and eighty feet high. The huge terraces were actually cube shaped hollow pillars filled with earth. An innovative chain pump system hidden from view was cleverly engineered to transport water from the east bank of the Euphrates River to the highest level of the terraced garden. Slaves were used to pull the chains and lift the water. The water then emptied, filtering down as a flowing stream, watering each layer of planted terrace. His beautiful young wife would sit and admire this wondrous beauty in a room he constructed especially for her. However, the desert air was hot and uncomfortable, and she was terribly unhappy. So the king designed a cooling system to lower the temperature of her sitting room, so she could sit and enjoy these lovely gardens. He redirected part of the water to flow into her sitting room, cascading gently down a stone wall. This effectively lowered the temperature of the room and lifted the spirits of his youthful wife. Nebuchadnezzar II could well be considered not only one of the earliest pioneers of hydroponics, but also one of the earliest innovators of water flow. This cooling technique has been used throughout the ages and is still a viable means of cooling greenhouse temperatures today. Not to be outdone, the highly gifted Aztecs of Central America were also early pioneers of hydroponics. Their development of floating rafts called Chinampas, were ingenious methods of growing plants along the shores of Lake Tenochtilan, an area located near present day Mexico City. These gigantic soil filled rafts were anchored by large poles or planted trees which prevented the Chinampa from floating away. Once planted, roots would grow through the rafts and into the lake, providing a steady supply of nutrition and moisture to the growing plants, today referred to as aquaponics. Quite large in size, Chinampas could be as wide as 35' x 300' in length, supplying a majority of the Aztec food.

This early hydroponics system somewhat resembled the non-circulating capillary method in this manual. Air, some type of aggregate anchor, in this case soil, and an abundant supply of nutritious water for healthy root growth, created a successful growing environment. Lake water provided huge amounts of oxygen as well as fertilizer. Other cultures have grown in water and documented their innovations. Ancient Chinese, Egyptians along the Nile and Aristotle in Greece to name a few. Growing in water, using soil only as an anchor support, is not new. The fundamental principles of air, water, and aggregate, along with some means of nutrients, have provided men with sustenance for countless ages. As far as the western scientific community is concerned, distinguished names like Dutchman chemist Jan Van Helmont (approx 1635), John

Woodward (approx. 1699), Jean Bousingault (approx. 1851), Julius Sachs and agrochemist Wilhem Knop,(approx. 1859-1865) were all credited with valuable evolutionary discoveries in the relationship of plants to soil and water. Van Helmont's 5 year experiment with willow shoots, although elementary by our standard, were innovative for his time. John Woodward, a fellow of the Royal Society of England, experimented with spearmint in distilled water, comparing it to impure water. His early papers lead to today's hydroponics, proving that water was the source of nutrients, even if they came from the soil. French chemist, Jean Bousingault discovered plants could grow in mediums such as sterile sand and charcoal, if they contained a well balanced nutritional solution. Germans Wilhem Knop and Julius von Sachs determined plants could live in a soil-less culture by incorporating the proper nutrients into the water they were grown in. Sachs is often referred to as 'The Father of Water Culture'. The term hydroponic is derived from the Greek translation meaning water (hydro) and labor (ponos), or literally, water working and came in the late 1920's and early 1930's from Dr. William Gericke, of the University of California. William Gericke, defined hydroponics, "as the art of crop production in liquid media." Dr. Gericke's important experiments using viable commercial agricultural plants used no other medium but water, in a true soil-less culture. It wasn't until agriculturalists became more aware of the disadvantages of soil such as weeds, diseases and soil fertility, that hydroponics moved out of academic levels into the commercial arena.

Today the term hydroponics includes the growth of plants in any inert medium, such as perlite, gravel or clay pellets, using only nutrient filled water as the source of nutrition. Men like Dennis Hoagland and Daniel Arnon (1933), although credited with developing a compre-hensive hydroponic solution that is still the basis of what's used today, also led to the development of subirrigation systems with aeration. This lead hydroponics to a commercial level of extensive aerated, circulating systems. A direction demanding elaborate and expensive designs available primarily to large scale commercialists or growers with sizable resources. For this reason, there is an urgent need for alternative systems.

Phillipines, 1985. Bernard A. Kratky, a horticulturalist from the University of Hawaii, and Dr. Hideo Imai, a Japanese scientist, were simultaneously spending time at the Asian Vegetable Research and Development Center in Taiwan. While watching the local farmers growing vegetables in the swampy, low lying land, they developed a theory.

Here were farmers planting into mounds of earth. Plant roots were extending into rows of standing water. How were these plants surviving? What agricultural principles were being applied to allow these plants the opportunity to flourish under these circumstances? Through careful observation, they considered what they saw. The upper portion of the plant's roots were being aerated, while the bottom half of the roots were left to sit in the standing water. The top half allowed the plant to survive. This hypothesis opened the door to the non-circulating hydroponic theory. If the upper portion of a plant's roots were left to aerate, while the bottom half of the roots were available for nutrition uptake, a plant could grow and flourish. Many studies and experiments followed. As you will learn, Professor B. A. Kratky's and Dr. Hideo Imai's extensive research has proven itself very effectively.

Bibb lettuce growing in non-circulating hydroponic beds. This greenhouse is covered with a 50% shade cloth placed over plastic. In Florida, shade cover was used in summer months and removed during winter. Great tasting lettuce with wonderful color.

NON-CIRCULATING HYDROPONIC THEORY

The hydroponic theory we will be applying should be referred to as the non-circulating capillary system. Sound intriguing? Let's see, non-circulating means we will not need to use any costly pumps to move and aerate the nutrient solution, no elaborate plumbing, and best of all no electrical power. Starting to sound even more interesting? It has been shown that plants can thrive if a well balanced portion of their roots are suspended into a nutrient solution, and an equal balance exposed to air, providing adequate aeration to the roots. This perfect balance of water and air allows us to grow plants without circulating water. The effectiveness of this is revealed on page 31, Exhibit 9. Note the healthy root structure and massive root growth.

Here you see a planted non-circulating hydro-bed with liquid nutrient producing strong healthy roots. The roots immersed in the nutrient solution are capillary roots. They provide an uptake of nutrients and water to the plant. The nutrient solution is specially fertilized water that the plants are grown in. What, in fact, is created, is a system providing adequate water, air and nutrients and is creatively applicable to various growing designs.

BUILDING YOUR SYSTEM

When choosing and designing your system, be imaginative. It should be a matter of individual preference based on your goals and resources. Outline your needs and create a realistic evaluation of your particular situation carefully considering basics such as what plants you are going to grow, available space, time, and finances. These factors relate to how your system is designed, constructed, and maintained. Don't hesitate to start small and expand as you feel comfortable. This manual will guide your successful hydroponic growing from a small or medium sized patio or backyard garden to a full scale commercial enterprise offering you an exciting and lucrative career. Whether you want to produce a salad for dinner or achieve financial freedom, applying these techniques will be a gratifying experience. In the last chapter we discussed the non-circulating theory. This was a good way to grasp the concept of hydroponic growing in a cost effective manner. We will now put that theory into practical application. This manual illustrates one type of growing design. Various alternatives to this design are explained and encouraged. You will see the effectiveness of the non-circulating theory in a real life commercial environment, and become inspired to choose a design that is suitable for you.

In this commercial setting, a series of non-circulating hydro-beds of 1" x 6" untreated pine were screwed together to form a 4' x 8' wooden frame. These were screwed onto a sheet of 4' x 8' -¾" plywood and set on cinder blocks. Refer to Exhibit 1. Perhaps you don't want a 4' x 8' hydro-bed. No problem. Any size, box or container, deep enough to hold your planted cup, while combining equal space for air and water, will work. Make your hydro-bed any size or dimension you like. Use plywood, other wood or purchase plastic boxes from a store. You could fabricate a metal or fiberglass hydro-bed or use a simple black plastic tub sold in the masonry department in large building supply stores. A five gallon bucket lined with black plastic works just as well and is perfect for tomatoes, peppers and even cucumbers. On the creative side, consider forming your own bed from layered cinder blocks or construct a smaller plastic lined box right on the ground, without any plywood bottom. This is great for cucumbers, or larger plants. Becoming more creative, you could use large PVC pipe by cutting holes for the planted containers and capping both ends. This can rest directly on the ground or suspend from an overhead support system. You can see there are multiple options available to you. Determine where you want to put your hydro-bed and remember the basic principles involved. You want a bed or tank to hold your nutrient solution and be able to suspend your growing plants.

Depending on the type of hydro-bed used, you will need a lining to retain the nutrient solution. Unless you have already purchased or built a black hydro-bed from the beginning, using a black lining in your hydro-bed may help to prevent the growth of algae. This is an important factor, since you want your nutrients feeding your vegetables, not algae. If you need to line your hydro-bed, consider the rolls of 6 ml black plastic sold at large building supply stores. Refer to Exhibit 2.

Lay the plastic evenly over your frame and begin to secure it to your hydro-bed. If your bed is made of wood, you can use building staples. If you are using a bucket, a large overhang will probably suffice. Make sure your plastic lines your hydro-bed completely, fitting squarely and snugly into its bottom and corners. Pond liners and any other black material that will hold the nutrient solution can be used. Don't hesitate to start with a small hydro-bed. Just remember, you need a strong enough frame to endure the weight of your hydro-top, rooted plants and water. Now let's think about the type of hydro-top you'll want. To reflect the sun and continue the prevention of algae consider choosing a white top for your hydro-system. Foam tops, although breakable, are relatively inexpensive and are found at most larger building supply stores. These 4' x 8' tops are easy to punch holes into for growing containers and cut down easily for any size hydro-bed.

Use the thinner grade of foam. This ensures roots have optimum aeration. Plywood is also an excellent choice and can be painted. Holes are harder to cut initially but provide a more durable and longer lasting hydro-top.

Exhibit 1.

Hydro-beds before plastic is put into place. A 4'x8' sheet of plywood with 4" sides, set on cinder blocks.

Exhibit 2

framed hydro-beds

Plastic lining stapled to the wood hydro-bed. These beds are capable of holding up to 52 heads of Bibb lettuce to full maturity. A closer spacing might jeopardize air flow resulting in fungus or other disease. Of course crop spacing is dependent on crop choice. Be sure plastic is evenly dispersed into corners.

The placement of holes in the hydro-top is very important, for now is the time you'll be deciding how much room your plants will have to develop and fully mature in growth. It is advisable to grow your lettuces, cucumbers and tomatoes in their own separate hydro-beds. If you choose to purchase the pre-mixed hydroponic fertilizers, there are separate fertilizers formulated especially for these vegetables. If you decide to use your own specific formula or one developed from another source, be sure it's a balanced formula for the crop you are growing. Most culinary herbs do not have their own premixed formula and depending on what herb you are growing can be coupled with the lettuce formula, or other available hydroponic fertilizers.

After choosing your top, decide what type of growing container you will use. Refer to the chapter 'Most Commonly Used Growing Containers' for help. This will determine hole size and placement. Now let's begin with the layout. Refer to the chart in the back of the manual for suggestions for particular crop spacing. Mark this onto your top and cut holes slightly smaller than the diameter of your container. Your container must fit snugly. Refer to Exhibit 3. If using foam, cut carefully so no breakage occurs. Take your time and be comfortable with your hole placement and hole size. It is always safer to stay a bit smaller, cutting away more later. One sheet of 4' x 8' foam is more than enough for several small hydro-beds. Circular cut outs of foam or plywood work well for your five gallon buckets.

Depending on the thickness, size and type of material used for your hydro-bed top, bracing may be required.

Exhibit 3

Braces can be strategically placed to balance the weight of the foam top and planted containers. Be careful to ensure braces don't interfere with holes cut in hydro-top for planting. Simple 1x2's are sufficient.

Exhibit 4

Styro-foam sheets are usually sold in 8'x10' increments. Be careful to build your hydro-bed frame in such a way as to leave a small shelf for this top to lay on. Once planted cups are in place, this lightweight sheet remains stationary. Styro-foam sheets may be purchased 1/2" or 1". The thicker foam is easier to work with and when wet, less breakage occurs however, it also provides less aeration. These sheets are relatively inexpensive but need replacing every few years. **Exhibit 5**

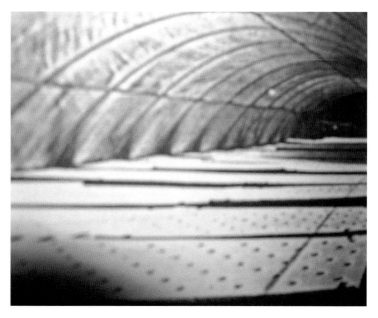

Be sure to place the braces to the inside of the hydro-bed, so your top will lay flat, carefully avoiding any holes you've cut out. It may be preferable to raise your hydro-bed off the ground. If planning a commercial venture, placing the hydro-bed frame on cinder blocks makes a very comfortable height to plastic line your bed, finish bracing and grow your vegetables. Any number of alternatives to cinder blocks can be used but remember the weight this hydro-bed will carry. A 4' x 8' hydro-bed holds 80 gallons of water. You will want to be sure your choice of legs will support this weight. Though requiring a bit more initial labor, construction and cost, raised beds prove more efficient later on in maintaining daily crop control in a commercial environment. Over a period of time, it makes planting, harvesting and general routine maintenance much easier. For the hobbyist, a plastic box on the floor of a patio or courtyard is just fine. Whether you build your hydro-bed directly on the ground or waist high, remember to keep your bed level. Before you begin to fill your hydro-bed with water, adjust this immediately. Stop the water 2" below the surface of your top. This will allow enough room for the container to breath, aerate the roots, and suspend the rooted plant in a nutrient solution to continue its growth.

Hydroponic crops require some type of covering. This covering must allow enough light to produce healthy plants, as in a greenhouse under clear plastic cover or on a well lit covered porch or patio. The objective is to keep the hydro-bed free from rainfall, maintaining proper nutrient level and pH control. It also help minimize disease and allows for a more controlled environment in general.

In Exhibit 6, simply constructed PVC framed mini greenhouses, placed directly on the ground work great. Smaller beds like these are excellent choices and can also be used for trials or familiarizing yourself before stepping into a larger greenhouse operation.

Exhibit 6

These mini-greenhouses can be done very in-expensively as no wood bottom is necessary. Level the ground and plastic line your hydro-bed frame, using the ground itself as its bottom.

MOST COMMONLY USED GROWING CONTAINERS AND HOLE PLACEMENT

• 10 – 12oz styro-foam cup (reuse as many times as possible)

• Plastic cup or pot (no previous holes)

• Any container you may invent, devise, or think up that does the job.

The styro-foam cup is highly effective, very cost efficient, and has a surprisingly durable shelf life. Although it's not biodegradable, it is reusable. In a small system, as well as a commercial one, it can do the job.

This type of cup is ideal for most plants. Transplanting into larger cups is feasible however you would need to enlarge your hole in the hydro-top affecting your spacing or change hydro-beds. Regardless of the container you choose to use, remember the basic principles of growing in a non- circulating system; a well balanced portion of a plant's roots must be suspended in the nutrient solution and an equal portion exposed to air, therefore providing adequate aeration to the roots. So choose the size of your growing container in accordance with your hydro-bed and top, switching beds as the plants get larger if necessary. To achieve this perfect balance of air and water, holes are needed in the container at particular positions. This step is rudimentary in the non-circulating system. Hard plastic containers can be drilled but be certain all plastic residue is cleared to avoid blockage. If using a styro-foam 10oz or similar size cup, four pencil point sized holes are drilled or punctured into the bottom of the cup. Four more holes are punched around the cup, approximately ½" up from the bottom and again, alternating, ¼" above that row. See Exhibit 7 & 8. One last row of five holes is made approximately 1" down from the top of the cup. The bottom holes allow the roots to grow through the cup into the nutrient solution, allowing for moisture uptake, the upper holes allow aeration. You will need to adjust this proportionately as your pot size increases. If you transplant, be sure your roots extend to the bottom of the pot when transplanting. Within days they will be growing out into the nutrient solution. As you can see, this truly is a simple growing technique, but as Exhibit 9 illustrates, an extremely effective one. Always keep in mind the basic principles of this non-circulating capillary system and choose containers that will meet these specifications. There must be bottom holes for the roots and upper holes for aeration, as well as fit securely into your growing system. No other holes! Your seedling or young plant is planted into this cup. Remember, when planted, your cup or pot needs to suspend into the nutrient solution. Hole placement is very important. Note the vigorous root growth in Exhibit 9.

Exhibit 7.

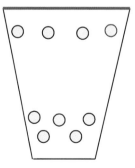

Exhibit 8

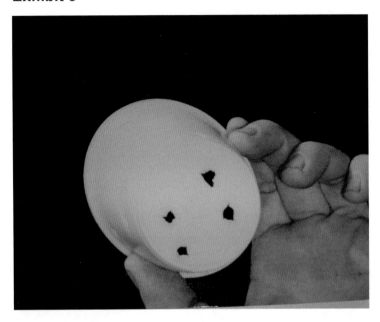

Exhibit 9

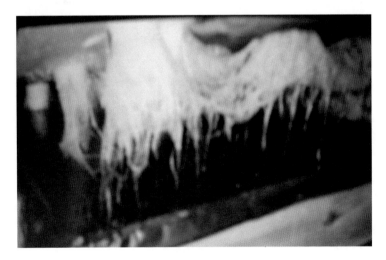

ANCHOR SUPPORT

Now that we understand the theory of non-circulating hydroponics let's add the plants. In a later chapter we will discuss the actual germination and cultivation of the seeds.
At this point let's focus on the growing environment of the roots. Plants will be grown in containers filled with an inert material herein referred to as media.

The inert media is typically composed of materials such as perlite or clay pellets which provide optimum aeration for root growth. The word 'inert' refers to a substance that does not in itself harbor any properties that aid in growing. It is basically a lifeless substance and cannot sustain a plant on its own. You must provide the nutrients for life and growth. Whichever media you choose, it must be porous in nature. Roots grow best in a loose media where water and air circulate freely. Most substances can be reused, even perlite. Avoid soil as this will flow through your container's holes, washing away the anchor support and contaminating the nutrient solution. Your media should be small enough, however, for the plant's roots to grab hold of and easily grow around. This hardy root growth and media combination create an anchor support that promotes strong, upright plant growth. Roots grow through the growing container down into the nutrient solution, becoming a capillary uptake of water and nutrients. The top half of the rooted media is suspended in the air. Now we see we have a healthy plant, growing in a partially submerged nutrient water base, with a hardy root system, in a small container. This demonstrates maximum plant growth and can be achieved using a minimum of materials within a self contained system.

SELECTING YOUR CROP

Determining what crops you'll be growing is fun and exciting and an important factor in designing your system. Some things to consider are light and space requirements as well as length of crop. If you are a relatively new grower, you may consider a fast growing crop, such as lettuce or other greens. Later, as you become more familiar with growing and growing techniques, a good balance would include your lettuces along with some European seedless cucumbers and some hybrid tomatoes and peppers.

These crops require more time and space. Lettuces and greens are hearty and fast growers. Refer to the section on seed propagation techniques to sprout your seeds and successfully grow young seedlings. Invest in hydroponic seed whenever possible. Refer to the section on material sources for references on where to purchase these. Non-hydroponic seeds can also be used with good results. Herbs are fun to grow and are a delight for the culinary artist in your home. It's also a lucrative crop. Most herb varieties do very well in the non-circulating hydroponic system. Basil is a particularly prolific grower. Arugala, cilantro, and greens such as endive are all excellent performers. Experiment with the varieties you like and see for yourself which do best. You will be amazed at the simplicity of growing successfully.

Establishing how much space you can devote to your garden will help you decide what to grow. It can be anything from a window sill, a portion of a patio or terrace, to commercial acreage. Remember though, your crop will need to be under some type of cover that also allows light. Patios and courtyards work well as long as they are covered. A small tub system can be built or bought with a minimum of expense and designed to fit into any well-lit space. It is prudent to note that some commercial hydroponic farming has progressed into the indoor arena, making available a large array of indoor grow lights for any location or size growing environment. There is virtually no location that cannot be accommodated as long as some type of power is available for your light. Remember, the beauty of this system is the fact that no electricity or alternative power is necessary for the actual growing of your crop. Here is some general information on the most commonly grown hydroponic crops:

Lettuces

Lettuces and most greens have a seed germination time of 2-3 days. Transplant seedlings in 7-14 days. Harvest maturely in approximately 30-45 days. Heading or romaine varieties usually take longer. If grown 6" on center or 2 plants per square foot, the average yield is 4-6oz per head. This is easily accomplished using the non-circulating method.

There are so many new varieties of lettuces and Mesclun mix seeds available, you will have trouble limiting your purchases once you begin. Experiment and decide which varieties you enjoy growing the most. Bibb lettuce is a hearty, rapid grower that is adored by chefs and is an excellent choice especially suited for commercial use. For personal consumption, this is an excellent staple. You can grow smaller amounts of your gourmet lettuces and herbs, creating a wonderful combination. Don't forget your medicinal herbs. There are brand new markets emerging for medicinal herbs and price per oz. can prove very rewarding. Send off for your catalogs, or look on line, and see what varieties are available to you

Basil

Basil is fun and exciting to grow. Its culinary purposes are numerous and its many varieties seem endless. Lemon, purple, Thai, sweet, sacred, West African, to name a few. You can enjoy fresh pesto as often as you like and sell all you can possibly grow to fine restaurants everywhere.

Cucumber

European seedless cucumbers have a germination time of 2 - 3 days. Seeds are expensive but expect an almost 100% germination. Plants require pruning and training. Leaves may reach a diameter of 12". Plants are usually grown upright, trained up heavy cord or overhead support wires using lateral growing techniques. Prune all lateral growth as plants begin to grow. A healthy plant must develop a strong root system, and this is achieved through early pruning. Remove all early flowers. Carefully train these plants using your lateral and overhead support system being careful not to break the fragile flowers. Fruit is allowed to grow when plants reach a height of approximately 3 feet or have grown at least ten true leaves. Plants can reach a height of 10' or more. Plant your seedlings into your hydroponic system 2 weeks after sowing, when plants have reached 10" or have grown 4 - 5 true leaves. During winter conditions, plants may take 5 - 6 weeks to harvest, 3 - 4 weeks during summer, depending on light conditions. Plants produce a 12 - 18" uniform green, bitter free cucumber, with a thin edible skin. Cucumber plants require 18 – 24" of space. Staggered apart, with an overhead support wire, trained in a V shape, they are heavy producers. With yields as much as 30lbs per plant from a 4 month crop. The average fruit weighs 1 lb. European cucumbers are a fast growing, high yielding and good primary crop. Keep in mind space requirements and pests in the summer months. Natural insecticidal soaps and organic dusts should be enough to keep plants healthy, should pest infestations occur. Exhibit 10 Cucumbers growing up support wires.

Tomatoes

Tomatoes can be fun as well as profitable to produce. Seed, used for greenhouse environments and field production are usually different. Plan your hydroponic tomatoes for either one long crop of 10 months or two shorter crops, factoring in your climate and light availability. Use clean sterile media and potting supplies. Seeds germinate best between 52 -72 degrees, usually within 3 – 10 days. Seedlings like to be watered with a light nutrient solution. Seeds are planted in 2" – 2 1/2" containers. Plants are usually transplanted at the 4 – 7 week stage, or after they have grown at least 4- 5 true leaves. Growing tomatoes requires half as much space as cucumbers, about 1 per square foot. It would be prudent to develop some growing experience before growing tomatoes. Remember, longer crops will require additional fertilizer along the way.

Tomatoes also require upright fastening of plants to overhead support wires. Plants can reach 10' or more in height and so require some plant management. Daily checks include nutrient conductivity, and pH levels. Inspect water levels and be aware of possible growing insect populations. An overhead support system of wire or twine is used to support and train the plants' growth. An estimated yield of 13lbs of quality fruit is not unreasonable, planted 2 plants per container, boasting a shelf life of 2-4 weeks under optimum conditions.

Tomatoes grown on the ground.

Tomato seedlings growing in an innova-tive hydro-bed.

There are many other vegetables you will be able to grow using the non-circulating hydroponics method such as hot or sweet peppers, both bell and banana pepper varieties, arugala, spinach or cilantro. Adjust your growing container to suit your crop. Experiment and explore. Soon you will be teaching your neighbors the principles of hydroponics and perhaps even earning extra income. One thing is certain, you will profit greatly from the joy of eating fresh vegetables and watching your efforts produce beautiful, healthy, living food. Please consider using healthy, organically or biologically derived pesticides. The opportunity to eat fresh, toxin free food is at your door step. With a minimum of effort you'll be growing your vegetables hydroponically and loving it, and possibly increasing your income at the same time.

PLANTING YOUR SEEDS GERMINATION AND TRANSPLANTING

Remember your primary objective when considering the best method for your seed production. Hydroponics is a unique, expeditious means of growing food. You may wish to incorporate only hydroponics in your growing arena. Certain seed, for instance, stakes its life strictly on water based culture. You may however, be bold enough to experiment, determining a personalized growing routine that incorporates soil to some degree. This portion of the manual is for you. Commercially, plastic cell packs or flats purchased at your wholesale nursery supply store can be used to sprout and grow your young seedlings. For the hobbyist, consider egg cartons. Most seeds prefer a small cell to get started, but using seedling flats is also effective. Once developed and strong enough to survive being transplanted, you will have an excellent rate of return. Nurture your seedlings and give them plenty of time to develop. Using only the strongest seedlings will ensure a healthy crop. Bibb lettuce is usually transplanted one plant per container. Monitor your sprouting so you don't over produce and waste seedlings. Also, be careful to avoid over planting your hydro-cups which will then produce smaller yields. Plants struggling for nutrients and space are usually small and weak. Fast paced production growing requires a streamlined operation. Develop a successful system and repeat this system each time you propagate and plant. Using soil to germinate your seeds, even your hydroponic seeds, is acceptable and should not be a deterrent. In the back of this manual you will find the addresses for commercial seed companies, offering hard to find varieties of vegetables as well as exotic herbs and companies providing all the growing supplies you will need to germinate and maintain your seedling operation. Remember you can purchase your seed in bulk and save leftovers from packets by placing in a jar with any type of silica or drying agent and place in the refrigerator.

Now let's get our materials ready for planting. If you've built a small hydro-bed, you won't need to purchase a large amount of seed and may prefer to buy young plants already started from your local garden center. These plants can be washed clean of soil and placed in your hydro-container along with your anchor support media and placed directly into your hydro-bed. Bam! You are ready to go. This is not the preferred way, but for some, it may be the only way you will successfully grow. These plants will grow hydroponically, although their seed is not bred for it. For a larger hydroponic operation, you will want to begin with hydroponic seed and if you are using soil to sprout, this next section is for you.

Consider the soil you'll be using. Ideally you want a quality soil mix especially formulated for seedling germination. You may need to contact a local grower, supply wholesaler or check online suppliers for soil products and prices. Your local garden shop may be able to special order a quality germinating mix from one of their suppliers. Otherwise, make do with what your local garden center carries. You never have to spend a lot or be inconvenienced to be successful, but using the right products will help you be consistently successful. Loosely fill your cell trays or flats. Brush excess soil away so each cell is visible or if using a flat, your soil is smooth and level. DO NOT PACK AND PRESS. The seed's roots will grow much faster in a loose environment. Dampen this soil prior to planting. Place your seeds on top of the soil. Unless you are planning a group planting such as a Mesclun mix, you will be transplanting only one seedling per hydro-container. Try not to overproduce when sprouting your seeds.

Very loosely cover your seeds with soil, and begin the process of keeping watch. These seedlings must be kept damp, yet stay warm. They can be eaten by mice or other rodents or develop fungus. Some growers cover them with meshed wire, and keep small grow lights on them at night to ensure a warm environment. Again, planting and seed choices are determined by your desired end result. This manual serves as a guide. Each grower will determine what is individually preferred and how to obtain those results. When germinating larger, hard shelled seeds, it is possible to sprout those indoors using wet paper towels on a plate. When sprouted, they can be planted into soil and grown with a 100% rate. Soaking your seed for the first night is also helpful.

You should begin to see germination during the allotted time. One method of letting you know its time to moisten your seeds is to place newspaper on top of the tray. If the paper appears to be drying out, you know its time to wet everything down. Remove the paper as soon as the seeds are sprouted. As your seedlings develop, be sure they get the proper sunlight. Too much sun as they sprout will cause them to dry out too quickly, but afterward, not enough light will cause them to appear lanky and spindly. So get them into the sun as soon as they are sprouted and then begin to water them with a weakened water soluble fertilizer solution. You will have stronger, healthier plants.

Germinated seedlings are ready to transplant when the roots are massed in the cell pack or there are roots extending to the bottom of the tray. At this time please read the chapter on fertilizer and nutritional requirements and prepare your bed with the nutritional solution. Seedling roots must be long enough to reach into the nutrient solution when planted. As soon as these roots are long enough, they can be planted. Remember your desired outcome and plant seedlings into your hydro-containers accordingly. Be very careful the roots are long enough to extend to the bottom of the container. Separate your seedlings when you are planting one per container. It is not necessary to have an overly developed root ball; this will develop as the seedling grows in the hydro-bed. These hardy plants can, however, be shocked by too much handling. Carefully hold your seedling over your hydro-container letting the roots fall to the bottom or near bottom of the cup. Pour your media into the container around the fine roots being careful to allow the roots to remain stationary. Place these planted hydro-containers into your hydro-bed which you have already prepared. Transplanted seedlings do best if misted for 3 – 5 minutes upon being placed in the hydro-bed. In warm or hot weather, regular misting should not harm the water level and will keep the plants from wilting. You will want to transplant in the latter part of the day to avoid heat stress. Refer to Exhibit 8. Remember, you want half of your hydro-cup submersed in the nutrient solution and half suspended in the air inside your enclosed bed. The bottom holes will allow for the uptake of nutrients and water and the upper portion will provide an environment for healthy root growth.

Lettuce seedlings ready to be transplanted into hydro-cups.

By keeping a constant supply of full grown seedlings on hand, crop rotation is maximized, and production can be streamlined. Lights are used in winter months to ensure proper temperature control. Notice plastic encasement. This wood frame supports plastic for enclosing the seedling box, maintaining a constant temperature in winter or whenever necessary.

FERTILIZER AND NUTRITIONAL REQUIREMENTS

Plants require carbon (C), oxygen (O), hydrogen (H), nitrogen (N), phosphorus (P), potassium (K), calcium (Ca), magnesium (Mg), sulfur (S), iron (Fe), boron (B), chlorine (Cl), copper (Cu), manganese (Mn), molybdinum(Mo), and zinc (Zn). The elements carbon, oxygen and hydrogen are, for the most part, supplied by the water and air. Nitrogen, phosphorus, potassium, calcium, magnesium and sulfur are elements that plants require a rather large amount of. Of course, each plant's requirements may vary slightly depending on size and variety, but you will find these elements must be abundantly present and are sometimes termed macro-elements or macro-nutrients. Iron, boron, chlorine, copper, manganese, molybdenum, and zinc are required elements, but are needed in much smaller quantities. These are commonly referred to as trace elements or micro-nutrients. Manufacturers of hydroponic fertilizer blends have developed complete fertilizers based upon scientific research and recommend the ratio and method in which to apply them. Using them is a good way to get started, experimenting with organic blends as you become more familiar with your plants' growing requirements. Being creative and making adjustments and refinements to these blends and ratios is possible, however be careful and experiment on a small scale first. If one applies the correct amount of nitrogen, following manufacturer recommendations, the correct amount of all other elements can also be applied. At this point, we could go into a detailed lesson of learning parts per million (ppm) per each nutrient added, however, fertilizer companies have simplified the concept. If you are growing standard garden vegetables, you need only to purchase an already formulated blend of fertilizer, which is a compound encompassing the majority of all the elements listed above. You can purchase this pre-mixed blend from one of the larger hydroponic supply companies. Refer to the Material Source section at the back of this manual. These commercial blends are formulated for specific crops, such as lettuce, tomato or cucumber. All are available pre-blended, but still require the same ratio addition of calcium nitrate, magnesium sulfate and potassium nitrate. For lettuces, greens and most herbs, use the Crop King hydro-blend of 8-10-36, which also contains major and minor trace elements. Your other crops will require a bit of a different balance of nitrogen, phosphorous and potassium or N-P-K, plus trace minerals. You will need to add calcium nitrate, magnesium sulfate and potassium nitrate to any hydro-blend. These minerals are found at most complete garden centers. An example ratio might be: 6oz. hydro-grow blend, 3oz. calcium nitrate, 1 ½ oz magnesium sulfate and 1/2 oz of potassium nitrate. This ratio is a basic formula to use regardless of the amount you'll be mixing. These ratios are adjusted according to the size of your hydro-beds. Manufacturer's recommendations should be followed, with formulas being adjusted for individual growing needs. Refer to the manufacturer's recommendations. If you are strictly organic minded, use the references at the back of the manual to find a supplier of organic blends. Organic farming should be seriously considered by any new hydroponic entrepreneur. This niche market is fast becoming the most lucrative of all agriculture markets. Check our web site for new information on organic blends for particular crops. In the mean time, contact organic hydroponic fertilizer suppliers for recommended products and ratios for particular crop requirements. It is very important to test your water at least once before adding your hydro-fertilizer. Everyone's water has a different pH level, and you will need to adjust this immediately, if necessary. There are inexpensive test kits available with suitable margins of error to adjust successfully if need be. Purchase a buffer solution of pH up or pH down from your local garden center to add to your hydro-bed to adjust the pH if your water's pH is too low or too high. When mixing your dry fertilizer into the hydro-bed, try funneling the dry fertilizer into a one gallon plastic jug or similar container, and then add enough water to shake and dissolve the fertilizer crystals. Fertilizer should be dissolved before being added to the hydro-bed. This fertilizer solution mixes very well in the 4x8 bed by itself, when applied dissolved. Here is an example to help your mixing breakdown. If one inch of water in a 4' x 8' hydro-bed = twenty gallons of water and for every twenty gallons of water, you use 1.5 oz. of hydro-fertilizer blend, 3/4 oz. of calcium nitrate, 3/8 oz of magnesium sulfate and 1/16 oz of potassium nitrate, then a 4' x 8' hydro-bed, using a 1" x 6" for side frames and a 4' x 8' plywood bottom, would use 4" of water or nutrient solution, which would equal 80 gallons of water. The ratio for this would be 6 oz. hydro-blend, 3 oz. calcium nitrate, 1.5 oz. magnesium sulfate and approximately 5/8 oz. of potassium nitrate. If constructing a hydro-bed smaller than 4" x 8", use the 1" per 20 gallons per 32 sq. ft. to calculate your own formula ratio. Short term crops usually require only one initial fertilizing. Fertilize longer crops using manufacturer's recommendations. By correctly calculating your hydro-bed fertilizer ratios your crops should be well fed during their entire growth process. If there are signs of fertilizer burn or you have pale, starving weak plants, salinity meters or conductivity meters may help determine the cause. You can always have your water or plants tested by one of the local laboratories to give you a true analysis of your situation. Check in the back of the manual under Material Sources for lab addresses. You can always drain your bed and remix the solution. Sending healthy as well as problem leaf samples and nutrient solution samples in for analysis, will give you a better understanding of your plants' particular requirements and if need be, recommendations for your particular environment. Test kits are available for home or commercial use. There are meters available that help you with your own analysis of pH and conductivity. By developing an awareness of your plants' needs, you will learn to prevent problems before they begin. You may find, especially on a small scale, you don't need to bother with lab analysis. Everyone's experience and growing conditions vary, these options are available to you should the need arise. The most important step to success will be your fertilizer blend calculations. Be as accurate as possible and you will produce healthy plants every time.

PEST CONTROL AND DISEASE CONTROL

Whether on a large scale or small scale you will usually find your first crops tend to give you the least problems. The longer the plants are in the same location, the more susceptible they become to pests and disease. Pest and disease control should be viewed as preventative in nature. Most common means of pest control is accomplished through spray programs and IPM or integrated pest management. Biodegradable and organically certified insecticides are available; see the chapter regarding Material Sources for places to purchase. On a small scale, using biodegradable dish soaps like Sunshine Dish detergent is recommended. This can also be mixed with isopropyl alcohol; 2TBS of dish soap plus ¼ cup of alcohol per gallon of water. Use as a good preventative weekly. Mix this soap/alcohol solution in a container and pour into a sprayer. It is much better to operate in a preventative manner from the start, in keeping your plants pest free. This spray is not harmful and will not interfere with the flavor or taste of the crop. Other home formulas like garlic and hot pepper sprays can also be effective. Commercial, naturally derived products such as Safer Insecticidal Soap or M-PEDE are also very effective. The most common pests you will encounter are the aphids, thrips, mites, caterpillars and leafhoppers. Insecticidal soap products work well on these pests. They clog the pores of the insect, forcing it to stop its life process while also sterilizing the plants killing fungus. Dipel, a product made from the bark of a tree, is sold commercially and recommended for Caterpillar control. Establishing a spray program early on will keep infestations down and provide an overall clean environment for your growing plants. If possible, be sure to use biodegradable, organic in nature, spray compounds. Be sure to cover the underside of the leaves as well, where most pests tend to live. Spray in the cool part of the day such as early evening when no rain is scheduled for at least 3 – 4 hours. There are a multitude of sprayers on the market to choose from. For a small home garden with only a few plants, use the plastic hand held spray bottles sold at garden centers. Invest in a good one as they tend to clog easily and should be cleaned with fresh water often. Also the pumps tend to give out on the cheaper ones. Backpack sprayers or 2½ gal. hand held sprayers with pump action are sufficient for most greenhouses, however, overhead injectors and foggers can be installed to minimize your labor significantly. Screening your growing area will prevent insects from entering, and although will not stop them 100%, does help. Use the bright, yellow, sticky paper sold at grower outlets. This inexpensive product is hung near the growing plants and helps to thin the insect population that is hovering about. Integrated pest management is an effective means of pest control, saving labor and equipment cost. Beneficial predatory insects are strategically released into the growing environment, preying on harmful pests. Your growing area must be enclosed or screened for best results. Do your homework, know which pests you are dealing with, and find the most effective predator for that pest. Research in this field is not conclusive, but enough is known to help the grower who is interested in establishing a balanced eco-system in his greenhouse. One method larger greenhouses practice is to first release the harmful pest, followed by the predator. Controlling the pest to predator ratio encourages healthy predator populations that are in place before natural pests move in. As an example, some predators like lady bugs and wasps are used to fight pests such as aphids and white fly. Remember, prevention is the name of the game. Creating a balanced environment where pests can't do destructive damage to your vegetable crops is the essence of pest control. Predatory insects are available through commercial suppliers, who are happy to provide you with the necessary information for your particular operation. Again refer to the addendum, Material Sources.

DISEASE CONTROL

Most plant diseases can be controlled through the same basic means as pest control. By using an effective spray control program and maintaining the overall health and cleanliness of plants and surroundings, you can be in command of your greenhouse environment. One of the most important items to keep in mind is general sanitation, through all steps of plant growth.

Most disease you encounter will be fungal, bacterial, or nutritional in origin. Air, water and physical transmission, as in touching diseased plants and then touching healthy ones, are all manners in which disease spreads. To control foliage fungus, watch for splash back from exterior water. Splashing or dripping contaminated water on your plants can lead to disease. Keep your growing area clean of weeds, and any other decaying plant matter. To control root fungus, make sure there is no algae build up in your hydro-bed and you have proper nutrient levels so roots are not burned, making them susceptible to root fungus. Leaf spotting, or chlorosis, may be fungal or bacterial. Bacteria play an important role in agriculture. A desired balance of good bacteria working in harmony to maintain a healthy equilibrium, both in the water, anchor support and on the plant is the objective. Careful observation will detect imbalances that if left unchecked will lead to poor yield, plant disease and possibly blight. The use of organic, biologically produced fungicides will help should an imbalance occur.

Nutritional deficiencies are also a catalyst for disease. Underfed, overfed, or food lacking in any one of the macro- or micro-nutrients, or elements, can begin a process of undermining a healthy plant. When these deficiencies are not addressed, the door to disease is opened. If your problem is of great concern you may want to send foliage samples to the lab for tissue analysis or empty the bed and begin fresh. Remember, there are alternatives to using harsh chemicals when treating these diseases.

The basic factor in maintaining proper disease control is to grow healthy plants by following good horticultural practices. A healthy plant is generally not likely to develop problems. Tips for healthy plant growth include: 1) Keep nutrient levels well balanced. 2) Keep plants as pest free as possible by removing disease or infested plants from your growing area immediately. 3) Observe your plants daily for the slightest signs of disease and treat the remaining plants with preventative measures. 4) Practice good clean sanitation, such as cleaning tools. Keep a weed free work and potting area, as well as weed free growing area. 5) Change gloves and wash hands often. 6) Refrain from introducing infested or diseased plants to begin with. 7) Establish a preventative maintenance program, and stick to it. 8) Keep a log of everything you do. Find what works, and repeat it again, and again. Use common sense regarding your particular operation and remember, a healthy plant will yield as expected. A stressed plant will be weakened and susceptible to pest and disease setbacks, reducing yields. If you have a problem you can't seem to get a grip on, start at the beginning, analyzing your entire growing process, step by step. To help you prevent future problems, get rid of sick plants and sterilize your growing area immediately, spraying surrounding areas with an alcohol mix, one part isopropyl alcohol to four parts water, or use M-Pede, following mixing instructions on the container. You can also seek professional advice by getting a nutritional, pest or disease analysis. Basically, a little prevention goes a long way.

These are hardy fast growing plants that, from healthy seedlings, want to produce a fine yield. There are organically derived fungicides and pesticides available which can help keep your problems to a minimum. Refer to the addendum on Material Sources for suppliers of these products as well as integrated pest management.

MARKETING

This chapter is for those interested in producing vegetables to sell on the wholesale level or directly to the consumer. You will be amazed at the attention your home grown vegetables will receive, from family, friends, neighbors and strangers. Producing garden fresh vegetables for yourself is rewarding enough, but having an abundance to share can be profitable. In a commercial operation, you may try publicizing a tour of your greenhouse or inviting a newspaper columnist or special feature writer over to do an article on your operation. This can provide the attention you deserve while explaining the benefits people will receive by using your products. Ads in local newspapers, mail-outs of fliers or brochures to potential customers, calling on restaurants and neighborhood groceries and yes, even a short ad on the local television station, could help increase attention producing positive results. Advertising your web address and providing

Information about your operation on your company's web site is a great way to lead potential customers to a better understanding of the products you're offering and secure sales. Operations large enough to obtain the attention of national food chains must persevere and you will gain results.

If your operation is smaller, a sign on the road or a well placed ad with a phone number may be all you need to find a market for the over-abundance of crops you're growing. Many times, friends and neighbors will provide enough business for your extra crops. Although growing with the pre-mixed hydro-blends is not organic, you can advertise pesticide free if you have not used toxic harmful pesticides. With some experimenting and product research, you can grow organically, entering into a very profitable niche. Be careful to obtain the correct certification before advertising on your products. One excellent market you can be sure will appreciate the fresh quality you're offering are the finer restaurants in town. These restaurants struggle for freshness. Basil, arugala, baby gourmet vegetables, and lettuces will turn heads and grab the attention of the busiest restaurant chef. Remember to bring samples with you and a business card or flier with your prices. Plan your visit during non rush hours. Chefs are surprisingly receptive. Always leave ample samples. Approaching produce managers of independent or smaller grocery chains is another means of marketing your produce. Most produce managers welcome fresh, well-packaged, quality products from local suppliers. Gourmet deli markets are also good venues, especially with gourmet variety produce that is neatly packaged. Other markets to pursue might be cafeterias, produce stands, hospitals, or wholesale produce distributors, who are listed in the yellow pages of your phone book. Call first and ask for the name of the contact person who purchases produce. Make an appointment if possible or ask when a convenient time to drop off a sample of your product and price list might be. Leave a good sized sample wherever you go, and be sure to make follow up calls. Some markets welcome the idea of setting up a sample display, promoting and educating the consumers on the advantages of buying hydroponically grown, locally fresh, pesticide free products. Food buying cooperatives are also a market you might want to consider. Following a combination of these methods, you should make all the contacts you need to stay sold out. Don't be afraid to call on new customers. More than likely you will find them happy to discuss your product, and eager to work with you. Don't become discouraged. There is a network of pleasant, easy to work with buyers in every town. You will find your own place in this market. You may even consider your own roadside stand. Remember, fresh produce has more of a demand now than ever before. There is an array of packaging materials available to enhance the appearance and marketability of your products. Head lettuces can be packaged in clear, hard plastic, shell containers while leaf lettuces can go in clear plastic produce bags, purchased from a product wholesaler. It is a good idea to feel out your projected markets and pricing before investing a lot in packaging. Lettuce can also be sold loose, by the case. Herbs can be sold in bunches, not necessarily bagged or boxed. Other products such as European cucumbers can be individually shrink-wrapped, either by hand or with the use of a small wrapping machine. Tomatoes may be boxed, sold loosely, or shrink-wrapped.

A brightly colored label with your business logo and product name is a good idea to draw attention to you and your pesticide free product. Commercial labels advertising 'gourmet quality' can be pre-printed and posted to your product. A few cents spent on packaging and labeling your product individualizes it and helps you get the price you need, as well as makes it a generally more marketable product and develops brand loyalty. This helps your customers build repeat business with the consumer. Be creative and have fun doing it. Your enthusiasm is your best asset.

**Draw a sketch of the hydro-bed
you're going to build.**

SPACING CHART (Not to Scale)

Lettuce

Cucumber

```
X    X      X    X

   X      X      X

X    X    X    X

   X     X    X

X    X    X    X

   X     X    X

X    X    X    X

   X     X       X
```

```
X


              X


X


              X
```

**With possible one
more**

Tomatoes

X

X

X

X

X

X

X

Draw your own

GLOSSARY OF WORDS YOU SHOULD KNOW

Aeration: The process by which a porous media allow water and air to circulate.

Anchor Support: A combination of the plant's root growth and inert media, such as perlite, uniting to form a strong support system for the plant's growth.

Bacterial: Plant disease sourced in micro-organisms.

Bibb lettuce: A heading lettuce with buttery tasting leaves well suited for hydroponics.

Biodegradable: Able to be recycled into the ecology.

Bio pesticide: A mixture derived from biological matter to kill unwanted insects.

Black light Trap: An infra-red device used in controlling pests.

Blight: Large scale infectious damage to living plants usually in a controlled environment.

Bolt: What happens to lettuce when it is going to seed.

Capillary: The portion of the plant's roots immersed in the nutrient solution providing an uptake of nutrients and water to the plant.

Chlorosis: Symptomatic yellowing of plant tissue. Yellowing of the leaves of a plant.

Conductivity Meter: An instrument which verifies the overall amounts of liquefied solids and determines the amount of dissolved salts.

Cultivation: The art of nurturing and growing of plants.

Disease: A disorder causing negative symptoms rooted in nutritional, environmental or biological causes.

Dipel: A derivative of Chrysanthemums that eradicates leaf worms effectively.

Elements: A matter that cannot be broken down in a chemical reaction, to any other substance.

Entomology: A scientist who studies insects.

Eradication: The suppression of and removal of an unwanted pest or disease.

Feeder root: A plant's roots that are the primary source of nutrients and water from the nutrient solution.

Fungal: Having to do with living micro-organisms, some beneficial, some which cause disease.

Fungicide: Usually of chemical origin, a liquid specifically designed to kill fungus.

Germination: The renewal of growth of a seed embryo into a growing plant.

Hosts: The living entity, as in a plant, that harbors harmful fungus or breeding insects.

Hybrid: The result of crossing one plant with another plant of a different species.

Hydro-bed: A formed and/or framed structure containing nutrient solution for growing plants.

Hydro-fertilizer: The mix of compounds needed to successfully grow plants in an aqueous growing environment.

Hydro-system: In this context, any technique using water to grow plants.

Hydro-top: A support structure for suspending containers of plants, into the nutritional solution of a hydro-bed.

Inert: Referring to a non living substance in which a plant is anchored and growing.

Infestation: A breeding mass of pests engulfing a part of a plant or plants.

Insecticidal Soap: A biologically safe spray that effectively treats most pests.

Insecticide: Chemicals produced to kill insects usually intended for pests.

Integrated Pest Management (IPM): Also referred to as Integrated Pest Control (IPC). A system of controlling harmful pests with regard to the environment, usually without using toxic chemicals. Also refers to the use of predatory insects against unwanted pests.

Layout: The spacing you choose between plants in your hydro-top.

M-Pede: A trademark for a widely used insecticidal soap.

Macro-element: A necessary element required in large amounts for the healthy growth of a plant.

Media: The substance used for containerized cultivation of plants.

Meters: Instruments designed to measure specific areas of greenhouse conditions as light, pH, concentrated salts in the nutrient solution.

Micro-element: A necessary element required in small amounts for the healthy growth of a plant.

Mist heads: Irrigation attachments used to produce the finest of sprays for cooling or wetting down of pant crops.

Mites: A resistant pest common to most vegetables.

NPK: The scientific abbreviation for the three of the basic requirements of plants: nitrogen, phosphorus, and potassium.

Nutrient solution: The liquid fertilizer and water blend that feeds your plants through their roots.

Overhead injectors: Irrigation allowing for the misting or treatment of a planted crop from above the plants.

pH: The scientific measure for alkaline or acidity in a solution.

Parasites: An organism living on or within another (the host) at the expense of the host.

Parasitoids: A wasp used as a biological control agent against leafminers like the Liriomyza sativae, a common pest to many vegetables.

Pathogen: An organism that causes disease.

Pest: Any organism that causes harm to humans, farm or nursery production.

Pesticide: Any substance used for the elimination or control of harmful pests.

Pesticide resistance: When pests are no longer controlled by a previously effective pesticide.

Porous: A substance that allows air or liquid to flow easily through it.

Resistance: The difficulty and resulting battle of certain pests or pest environments to treatment.

Rot: The end process of diseased plants as they decompose.

Rust: A fungus that causes disease to plants. Symptoms are orange / brown in color.

Scorch: Burning of a plant's leaves due to the sun.

Shelf Life: Length of time a product is able to remain in storage and still be effective in use.

Spot Treatment: Application of a remedy (as a pesticide or fungicide) to a portion of plants in your growing area.

Swath: The action and area of treatment when using a sprayer, handheld or backpack.

Symptoms: A visual indication of irregularity with a growing plant or plants.

Tolerance: A built up immunity to certain treatments by pests or plants.

Toxic: Extremely harmful to humans, usually referring to a chemical.

Trace elements: Necessary elements required for a plant's growth in minute amounts. (same as micro-nutrients)

Viable: A possible and usually practical means of accomplishing your objective.

Weed: Any undesirable plant in a given location.

Wilt: The loss of water in a plant's leaves that cause it to fall downward and droop.

If you 're new to agriculture, becoming familiar with the terminology will help you understand and participate in the dialog, enabling you to explain yourself when describing a certain situation or need. These are common definitions that will acquaint you with some of the industry's general terms and commonly used by other growers. These definitions are not intended to be all inclusive.

MATERIAL SOURCES
Just a few to get you started.

- Informational Material

Simply Hydroponics
www.simplyhydro.com

Practical Hydroponics & Greenhouses – Magazine
www.hydroponics.com.au

Greencoast Hydroponics
gchydro.com

Type in hydroponics; non-circulating hydroponics; hydroponic supplies; hydroponic catalogs, on the internet and discover more for yourself. Also search "Bernard Kratky," University of Hawaii, Manoa; teacher and developer of non-circulating hydroponic systems.

- Hydroponic Growing Fertilizers

Crop King
www.cropking.com
330-302-4203

Hydrofarm
www.hydrofarm.com

Worm's Way
www.wormsway.com
1-800-274-9676

Eco Enterprises
www.ecogrow.com
800-426-6937

Sunshine Supply Hydroponics
www.sunshinesupplyhydro.net
407-859-7728

Atlantis Hydroponics
www.atlantishydroponics.com
888-305-4450

- Seedling Growing Supplies – Cell packs, seedling soil mixes

B&T Grower Supply
www.growersupply.com
800-748-6487

Gardeners Supply Company
www.gardeners.com
888-833-1412

International Horticultural Tech. LLC
www.ihort.com
831-637-1800

- Seeds

Crop King – Hydroponic
www.cropking.com
330-302-4203

The Cooks Garden – Not hydroponic
www.cooksgarden.com

Organica Seed Company- Not hydroponic
www.organicaseed.com
413-599-0396

Richters
www.richters.com
905-640-6677
Specialty Herb Seeds
Not hydroponic but great selection and they work.

- Natural Pesticides and Treatments

Eco-grow
www.ecogrow.com
800-426-6937

Worm's Way Catalog
www.wormsway.com

Sunshine Hydroponics Garden Center Catalog
www.sunshinehydro.com
888-833-4769

- Integrated Pest Management

Crop King (search Beneficials)
www.cropking.com
330-769-202

Urban Sunshine
www.urbansunshine.com
888-837-47469

http://www.epa.gov/opp00001/factsheets/ipm.htm

- Meters and Instruments

Worm's Way Catalog
www.wormsway.com

Sunshine Hydroponics Garden Center Catalog
www.sunshinehydro.com
888-833-4789

Gemplers
www.gemplers.com
800-382-8473

Lots of places online, check out growing supplies and hydroponic supplies.

- Greenhouse Manufacturers & Kits

BWI –professional growers
bwicatalog.bwicompanies.com
Cold frame greenhouses
Corp. office -903-838-8561
Call for nearest location.

C & P Enterprises
Apopka, FL
407-886-3321

- Laboratories

A & L Labs
www.allabs.com
800-264-4522

- Additional Supplies

Home Depot (or any building supply store) –
sheets of white foam, rolls of black plastic for lining,
staples, staple gun, plywood, 1" x 4's.

Any Wholesale Restaurant Supply Co.
10 oz styro-foam cups

REFERENCES

History of Hydroponics. (2001, September 29). http://archimedes.galilei.com/raiar/histhydr.html.

History of Hydroponics. (1999, April 12). http://www.k12.hi.us/-ckuroda/history_of_hydroponics.html

IPM Gempler's Almanac (2005). http://www.gemplers.com

Jensen, Merle H. (1997, October). Hydroponics.*HortScience, Vol.32(6).*

Kratky, B.A. (1996). Non-Circulating Hydroponic Methods. *DPL Hawaii, PO Box 6961, Hilo Hawaii 96720.*

Kratky, B. A., Bowen, J. E., Imai, H. (1988). Observations on a non-circulating hydroponic system for tomato production. *HortScience 23(5):906-907.*

Osborne, L.S.; Pettit, F.L.; Landa, Z; Hoelmer; K.A. Biological control of pests attacking crops grown in protected culture: the Florida experience.Pest Management in the Subtropics, Biological Control – a Florida Perspective Intercept Ltd, Andover, Hampshire SP10 1YG, UK

Petitt, Frederick L. (1996, November). Biological Control and Integrated Pest Management at the Land, Epcot. *Presented at Eco-Informa, Lake Buena Vista, Florida.*

REFERENCES

Seminario #8. (1997). *Centro Historico.*
Cuauhtemor, Mexico, D.F. 06060 Museo del Templo
Mayor. Institulo Nacialonal de Antropolgia e Historia,
Mexico. http://www.wikipedia.com

The History and Future of Hydroponics. (1999).
Irrigation Journal-Jul/Aug.
http://www.greenindustry.com/ij/1999/0899/899hydro.asp

41203954R00055

Made in the USA
Lexington, KY
03 May 2015